Beetles

CLAIRE LLEWELLYN • BARRIE WATTS

W
FRANKLIN WATTS
LONDON•SYDNEY

This edition 2004

Franklin Watts
96 Leonard Street
London
EC2A 4XD

Franklin Watts Australia
45–51 Huntley Street
Alexandria
NSW 2015

Text and artwork © 2001 Franklin Watts
Photography © 2001 Barrie Watts,
except page 18: John Cooke © Oxford Scientific Films

Series editor: Anderley Moore
Editor: Rosalind Beckman
Series designer: Jason Anscomb
Illustrator: David Burroughs

A CIP catalogue record is available
from the British Library.
Dewey Classification 595.4

ISBN 0 7496 5210 1

Printed in Hong Kong/China

Contents

What are beetles?

This large beetle has strong jaws.

Beetles are a kind of insect. There are so many different insects that scientists have sorted them into groups. Beetles are the largest insect group of all. There are over 400,000 different kinds.

Beetles come in
many colours,
shapes and sizes.
Most of them are
black or brown,
but some
are golden
or bright like jewels. Beetles
can be long and slim, or
dumpy and round.

You often see
beetles scurrying
along the ground
in gardens, woods
and parks. You
also see them
crawling up plants
or flying through
the air.

▲
This goliath beetle is
bigger than your hand.

▲
A brightly-coloured leaf chafer.

Where do they live?

Beetles can live almost anywhere on earth. They live on high mountain peaks, in hot, wet rainforests, dry deserts and the icy Arctic. Beetles that live in the Arctic can only survive in places where plants will grow.

Rainforests are home to thousands of different sorts of beetle. Sometimes there may be over 100 different beetles on a single tree!

Some beetles can survive in hot, dry deserts. Their waxy, waterproof skin keeps them from drying up. They usually come out to feed at dusk when it is cool.

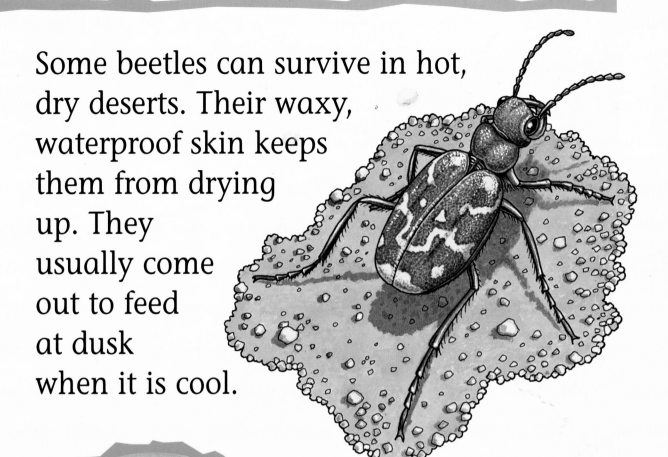

The tiger beetle lives in hot, dry places.

Some beetles live in water – in rivers, lakes and ponds. The one place beetles do not live in is the salty sea.

The great diving beetle lives underwater.

A beetle's body

Like all insects, beetles have three parts to their body: the head, the thorax and the abdomen. They also have three pairs of legs. On the outside of their body is the exoskeleton. This is like a tough case which protects their soft body.

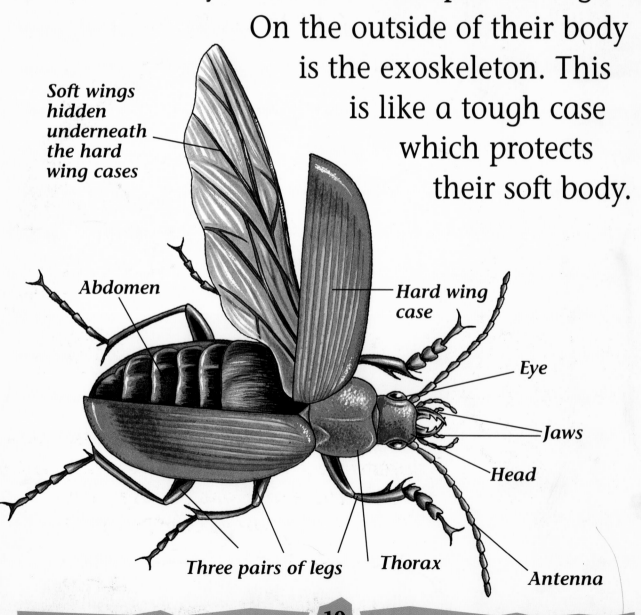

Soft wings hidden underneath the hard wing cases

Abdomen

Hard wing case

Eye

Jaws

Head

Three pairs of legs

Thorax

Antenna

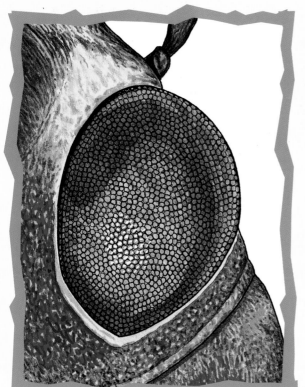

Beetles have two compound eyes. Compound eyes are made up of many different lenses. Each lens sees just a small part of the picture, like one tiny piece of a mosaic.

Some beetles have long legs that help them to run fast over the ground. Tiny bristles on their feet help them to grip glossy leaves and other slippery surfaces.

The longhorn beetle has long, feathery antennae. A beetle's antennae help it to touch, taste and smell things, and pick up movements in the air.

Beetles that fly

Flying is a quick and easy way for beetles to escape from danger. It also helps them to look more widely for food or a mate.

▲
A cockchafer in flight.

Large beetles make a humming noise with their wings. They are rather clumsy fliers.

Beetles have two pairs of wings. The front pair are hard wing cases. These protect the larger back pair, which are delicate and folded out of sight.

A cockchafer beetle prepares to fly.

❶ **The beetle crawls to the top of a plant and gets ready for take-off.**

❷ *It opens and closes its wing cases once or twice to warm them.*

❸ *Now the beetle spreads out its wing cases and the back wings begin to unfold.*

❹ *The beetle jumps off the plant, beats its back wings strongly, and drives itself forwards through the air.*

Feeding on meat

Some beetles are fierce hunters. They eat many small creatures such as caterpillars, snails, slugs and ants. Many of these animals are pests that spoil food crops and other plants.

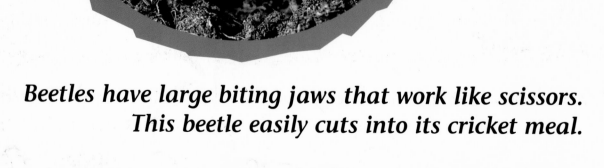

By eating the pests, beetles help farmers and gardeners to protect their plants.

Beetles have large biting jaws that work like scissors. This beetle easily cuts into its cricket meal.

Many beetles feed on the rotting remains of dead animals. As they feed, the beetles help to break down an animal's body and mix it in with the soil. This feeds the soil and helps plants to grow.

Some beetles feed on animal dung. This is helpful because it gets rid of the mucky waste and flies, which spread disease.

Dung beetles feed on different kinds of dung – from small rabbit droppings to huge piles of elephant dung!

Feeding on plants

Not all beetles are meat-eaters; many of them feed on plants. They munch a plant's green leaves and stalks, or drink its juicy sap. Sometimes you see beetles crawling over flowers. They feed on the fine, yellow dust called pollen, and the sweet-smelling drops of nectar.

◀ *As beetles feed, they spread pollen from one flower to another. This helps plants to make seeds.*

Some beetles feed on farm crops and are real pests. Weevils are a large group of crop-eating beetles. Each kind of weevil has its favourite plant – carrots, apples or cotton plants – or grains, such as wheat and rice.

The tropical weevil uses its long snout to ▶ *drill into its food.*

◀ *Some beetles, like this carpet beetle, are pests in the home.*

Finding a mate

Before female beetles can lay eggs they need to mate with a male. Finding a mate can be difficult because most beetles live on their own. They have to send out signals to other beetles near by.

A female glow-worm signals to males by flashing a light on her abdomen.

Some beetles signal with light or sound; others use a strong-smelling scent.

Sometimes two male beetles will fight over a female. A male stag beetle uses its huge jaws to pick up a rival, carry him off and flip him on to his back! The winning beetle then hurries back to the female to mate.

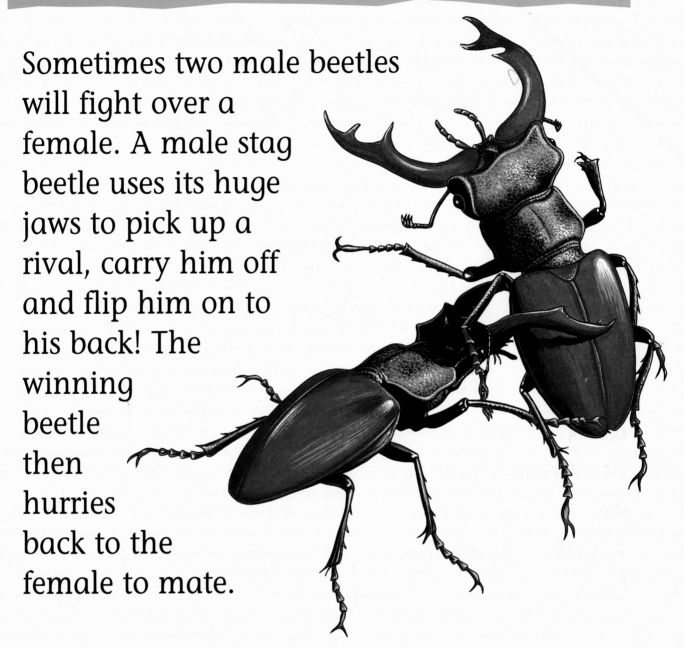

The stag beetle's jaws may look fierce but they are quite weak. They do very little harm.

The deathwatch beetle calls for a mate by drumming on wood with its head and creating a loud ticking sound.

Laying eggs

Like many insects, beetles go through four different stages as they grow. These four stages make up a beetle's life cycle. A beetle always lays its eggs near food. Then, when the eggs hatch out, the young have something to eat.

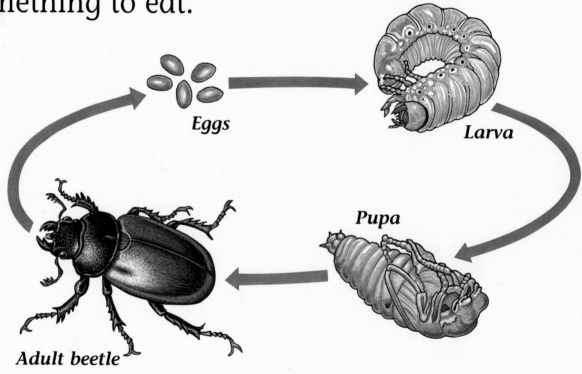

Eggs

Larva

Pupa

Adult beetle

The life cycle of the stag beetle.

The larvae, or grubs, that hatch out of a beetle's eggs look nothing like their parents. Many of them live hidden away inside rotten tree trunks or under the soil.

The newly-hatched larvae of the mealworm beetle look like tiny worms.

Woodworm, the grub of the furniture beetle, makes holes in floorboards, doors and roof timbers. It turns good wood to dust.

Body changes

A beetle larva starts to eat as soon as it hatches from the egg. It grows quickly. Soon its body gets so big that its tough skin starts to split. Under the old skin is a new, softer skin with plenty of room to grow. This is known as moulting and it happens several times in a larva's life.

As they feed, the larvae grow much bigger and fatter.

A mealworm beetle changes from larva to adult

1 **When the larva is fully grown, it stops feeding, moults once more and changes into a pupa.**

2 **Inside the pupa its body starts to change.**

The different stages in a beetle's life cycle last from a few days to several years. A cockchafer beetle spends three or more years as a larva, but only a few months as an adult.

3 **A few weeks later, the pupa splits open and an adult beetle crawls out.**

Staying alive

A beetle has many enemies. It may be eaten by birds, lizards or small mammals such as shrews. But beetles have ways of defending themselves. Their small size helps them to hide away and keep out of sight. Also, most beetles can fly away quickly.

Shrews are great insect-eaters. They hunt for beetles among dead leaves on the ground.

Some markings work as a warning. The bright colour and spots on a ladybird warn birds that it tastes very bad.

The colour and markings of some beetles are another kind of defence. Camouflage helps them to blend in with their background, making them harder to see.

The colour of the ▶ longhorn beetle blends in with the rock.

◀ A green tortoise beetle is hard to see on a leaf.

Beetlemania

The world's heaviest beetle is the Goliath beetle of Africa. It weighs up to 100 g – that's as heavy as a hamster.

The smallest beetle is the feather-winged beetle. You could fit four on the head of a pin.

When cows were first farmed in Australia, there were no native beetles to clear up their dung. Dung beetles were brought from Africa to clear up all the mess.

Dung beetles can find a pile of fresh dung 60 seconds after it has hit the ground!

The longest beetle is the Hercules beetle. It is 15 cm long – about the size of an adult's hand.

Glow-worms were once used as reading lamps. Their glow lasts for about two hours.

In Japan, stag beetles are often kept as pets. They are very expensive to buy.

In some parts of the world people eat beetle grubs as a snack. They roast them or eat them raw.

Water beetles have long, hairy fringes on their legs to help them paddle through the water.

In Ancient Egypt, the dung beetle was the symbol for the Sun god, who rolled the Sun across the sky each day.

Glossary

Abdomen   The last of the three parts of an insect's body.

Antenna   One of the two feelers on a beetle's head. (Plural: antennae)

Compound eye   An eye made up from many different lenses (the parts of the eye that help animals to see).

Exoskeleton   The tough, outer coat that protects the body of insects and other small animals.

Insect   An animal with three parts to its body and three pairs of legs.

Larva   The young stage of an insect after it hatches out of an egg. Beetle larvae are often called grubs. (Plural: larvae)

Life cycle   All the different stages that an animal goes through in life, until it has its own young.

Moult   To shed an old skin in order to make way for a new one.

Pupa   The stage in an insect's life when it changes from a larva to an adult. (Plural: pupae)

Thorax   The middle part of an insect's body, in between the head and the abdomen.

Index

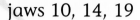

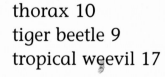

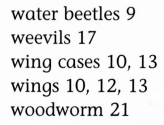